Ramadan
Coloring Book
FOR MUSLIM KIDS

70 Pages of 8 x 10 in

This book belongs to:

....

....

....

Ramadan Kareem

Ramadan

Ramadan

Ramadan

Ramadan

Ramadan

Ramadan

RAMADAN

Ramadan

Ramadan

RAMADAN

Ramadan

Ramadan

Ramadan

Ramadan

RAMADAN

Ramadan

Ramadan

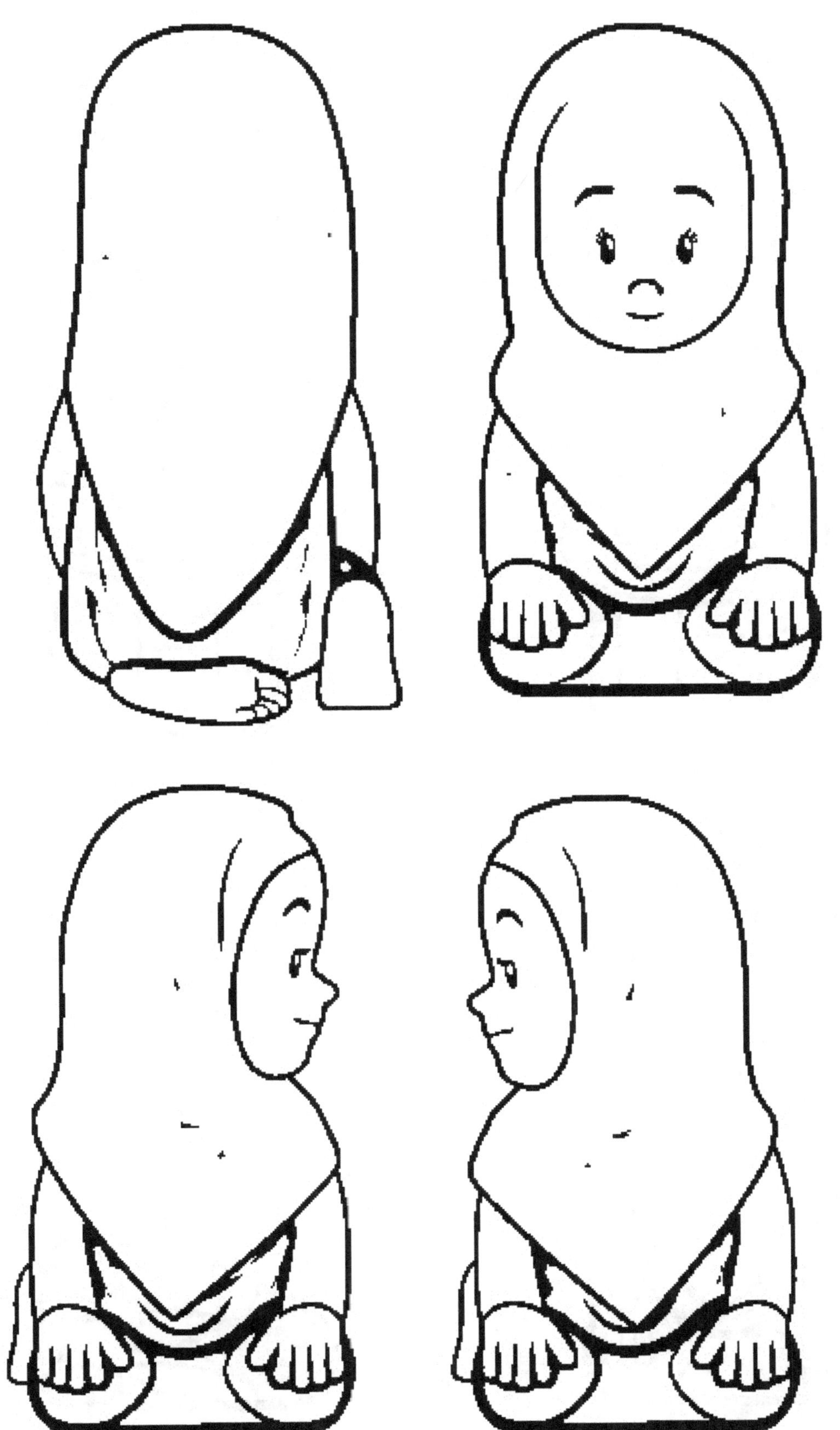

سبحان الله

بِسْمِ اللهِ الرَّحْمٰنِ الرَّحِيمِ

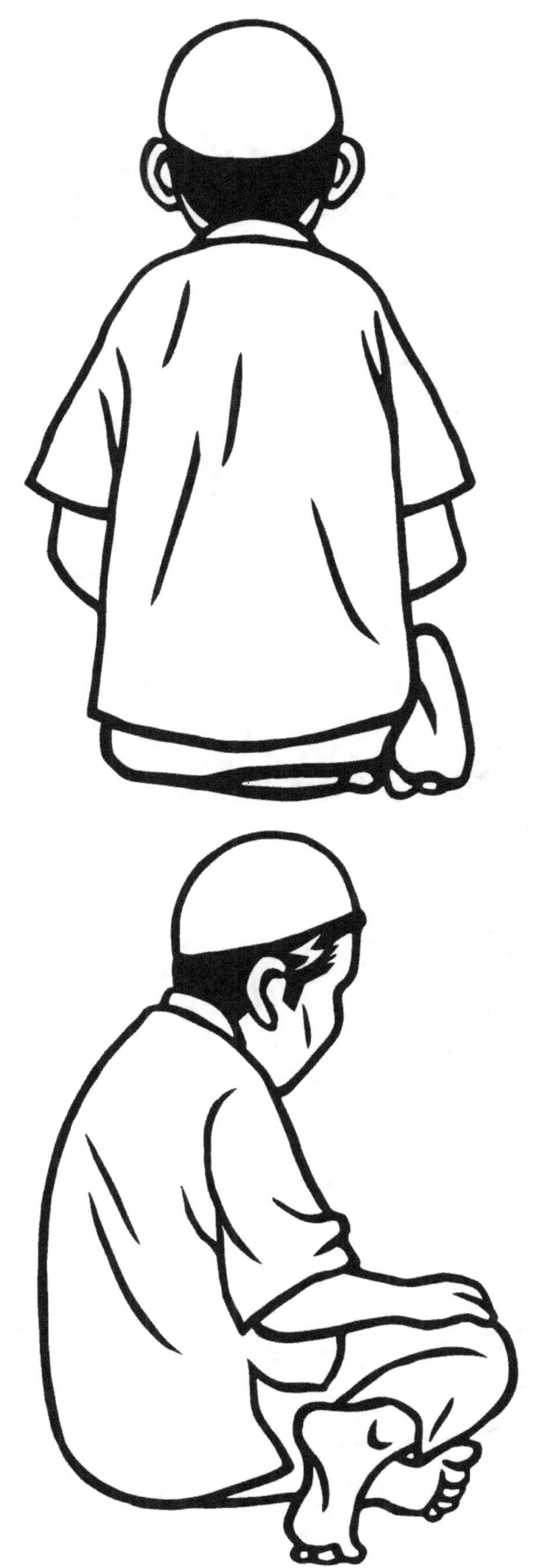

Ramadan

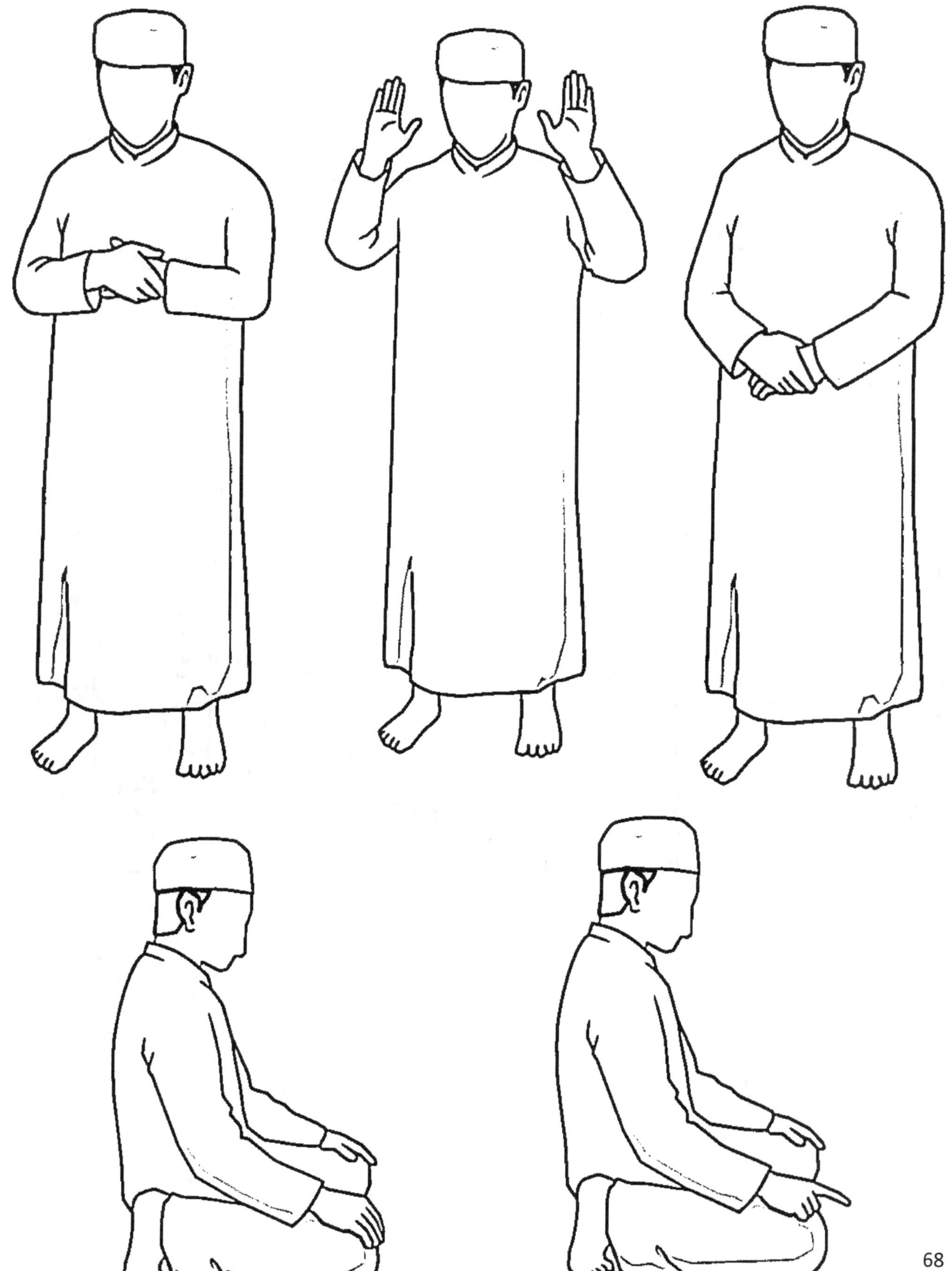

Ramadan Kareem

الحمد لله ربي العالمين

«Alhamdou lilaahi rabbi l-aalamiine »

Praise be to Allah, Lord of the worlds

Please, if you have any remark, don't hesitate to contact
us via this e-mail: apamog@hotmail.com

* 9 7 9 8 7 2 4 7 0 9 3 9 2 *